FORTY-FIVE MINUTES IN CHINA

FORTY-FIVE MINUTES IN CHINA

Rowland Evans

Terra Nova Publications

First published in Great Britain in 2005 by
Terra Nova Publications International Ltd
PO Box 2400, Bradford on Avon, Wiltshire BA15 2YN

Registered Office (not for trade):
21 St Thomas Street, Bristol BS1 6JS

Cover design by Roger Judd

ISBN 1 90194 939 7

Printed in Great Britain
by Bookmarque Ltd, Croydon

Contents

Foreword

Are you sitting comfortably? Then don't read this book! You will begin with pleasure but finish in pain.

It is *poetic*. This Welshman is a master of the English language. The descriptive style is brilliantly written, a delight to the mind. China comes alive in a vivid way. Rowland takes you with him on his travels. But the literary sweetness disguises strong medicine which leaves a sour taste.

Because it is also *prophetic*, in three particulars. First, China is rapidly becoming the next world super-power, which will affect all of us. Second, just as the industrial revolution enriched the few and impoverished the many, so the technological creates a widening gulf between the haves and the have-nots. Third, society will become increasingly hostile to Christians, until they are hated by all nations, as Jesus predicted.

Rowland is a practical man, a motivator of others. I know he has only one objective in putting his pen to paper: to leave the readers wanting to be involved and asking the Lord what He wants them to *do* about it. I had to do this after reading it (in one sitting).

First, I knew I must write this Foreword. I had hesitated when requested to do so, partly because my contacts with the author have been infrequent and my knowledge of his mission limited, but mainly because I felt totally unworthy to be linked with his amazing ministry. However, if my name would help to bring that to wider notice, I felt I could not decline.

Second, we had already begun to translate my tapes and books, and to dub my videos, into Mandarin, thankfully now replacing the many different dialects. The great need of the Chinese church is for balanced biblical teaching to stabilise and mature their millions of converts. I am now more determined than ever to pursue this task.

Will you dare to read it, knowing what could result? You might even find yourself in China itself, as one of those the author calls 'my colleagues'.

You have been warned!

David Pawson

To our granddaughters
Lauren, Hannah and Zoe
who have, from both sets of grandparents,
a missionary heritage from China

Introduction

A shark hangs in the sky–clear sea mere inches from my hand, still, apart from a steel cold restless eye that misses nothing of my movement. In the steamy heat I shiver involuntarily. I cannot work out if a source of primal fear in me projects a terrifying reputation onto the creature, or if it truly deserves it. Either way I am relieved that the moving walkway carries me away through a glass tunnel along a simulated seabed, far from the frightening intention captured in that evil eye.

In minutes I emerge into the real world, under the dome of an indigo sky and a sun that is taking its bow on the western rim. The moisture-laden breeze, heavy with the scent of a tropical sea, bathes away the stress of a high tech day, and Singapore's fantasia of sight and sound awakens with the dusk. Against a backdrop of cascading water, light and laser play to a rendering of Mozart's requiem. I am enthralled.

The monorail that encircles Santosa Island has closed, so a pleasant walk in the sea–spiced night air encourages me to breathe deeply and relax, and the lights of the city arch across the sky.

* * *

Familiar landmarks flashed into view through the window of a bus in the efficient transport network. The next stage would return me to my lodgings. The pressed shirt and neat appearance of the driver impressed me, as did his keen eye that caught my hesitation at the auto ticket machine. In a millisecond his fingers spell out the fare. Neither had I failed to notice the painted banner he had stretched across the front of his vehicle. In bold words, it spelt out:

I am proud to drive this bus.

* * *

A familiar frustration invades the privacy of my pleasurable world of memory, and I am torn away from Singapore to the reality of a crumbling Mao-era building in a small town in south west China.

I look down from a first floor window on a bus thick porridge of traffic below. It roars its toxic fumes into the morning air, cyclists wear masks, and tissues hide pedestrian faces, and all with blood-red eyes.

The frustration that returns to antagonise me lies in my failure to be able to answer the simple frequently asked question, 'How is China?' I am steadily losing faith in my well-rehearsed and polished thirty second response, which I hoped would both satisfy the enquirer and mask my own confusion.

A decade ago an avalanche of cyclists and trishaw riders would have poured along the same route, where in fifteen minutes I had counted a staggering hundred buses of varying styles and sizes. Conductors hang from open windows, calling their destination to the pavements heaving with workers. The street forks, and to the accompaniment of a cacophony of squealing brakes and growling gears they jostle for position, only minimal air space separating them.

From the neck of the street from which the sticky, thick flow issues, sounds a wildly discordant note. A pall of black smoke identifies its source: a small bus, its appearance making no attempt to disguise its age, and a driver not hiding the fact that he is making an all out effort in the massed start sprint to the fork in the road. Its straining diesel engine – starved of the oxygen its wheezing lungs fail to scour from the polluted air – blasts out unburnt fuel clouds which fall as soot-black mist.

I am about to turn away when a slip of the eye frames its driver. Both pilot and navigator in one, with a vehicle too old for the ease of power steering, he stands over an enormous wheel and hauls his passengers away from a certain collision.

It is then I notice the hand-painted words on the side of the bus:

All this thins are belong to me

I think I understand the glow of pride that lights his face. This wrestling hero is a thin man, his crumpled shirt wet with perspiration, his features set by hidden strength, his bow-strung muscles rippling with the spirit of China. He is a man sure of what he hopes for.

China is many things lived to the extreme ends of life. Simple answers are as complicated as the misspelt words on the side of the bus. Confusion lies somewhere within most signals. This sorrow I think I carry in my heart. I have to admit that the following brief chapters may hold no more insight than a momentary stray reflection from a shattered looking glass. For sometimes it feels as if life for me is no more than a faint etching on the surface of the mystery called China.

* * *

I receive an email from a Chinese school teacher colleague whose parents were at one time under the orders of the Red Guard to leave the town for the country to work in the fields. It reads, 'My parents and I often miss you.' It is worth a million pounds.

China

This is China, though not the China I really love, where imagination unbridled can assault white-mantled mountains whose defences reach for the sky. Terrifying, they stand in their stark jagged outline, towering above river gorges, terraced hillsides and mud-daubed villages. The China where solemn dark pagodas of ancient monasteries claim the last inch of a bare frozen rock outcrop —defiantly they stand as they have done for centuries, the land sweeping away before them in every direction. To reach them, a significant effort; to live and die there unimaginable.

Or the dreamlike landscape of columnar mountains. A forest of odd shaped cathedral spires of irregular heights and at irregular intervals. They cast their yellow and brown reflections in the sea of lake or river. Drifting spray from cascades that have carved the limestone into steps and gullies bring dramatic, surreal beauty to clusters of fisher families' huts and the solitary water buffalo, with ringed snout and halter, that simply stands and stares.

Gnarled trees that grow from crevices in the high cliffs and the luscious green fern, their abundant, feathery foliage moving slowly to the rhythm of the eternal swirling mists, surround with mystery the dark figure on the rock slab shore.

He is tall and thin, dressed in a simple, deep blue smock with knee length trousers. He wears a wide-brimmed hat, pulled tightly to his head. He is barefoot, and his ease of movement over the rock shows that this is what he prefers. He seems to be busying himself, launching a long narrow raft of bamboo poles lashed together. It has a crude box fitted towards the stern, and with a long bamboo pole he makes distance between the craft and the shore. Strangest of all are the passengers that crowd the foredeck. They are a line of long-beaked, large, black water birds, their elegant necks metal-ringed, each with a tether which fastens them to the craft. Their feathery unrest is soon rewarded as the boatman strikes the foredeck with his long pole and the birds dive under the water. As they flap their wet bodies back onto the deck, each has a struggling fish protruding from its gullet. In turn, the boatman holds each upside down until the fish drop into the wicker box near the stern. Before the mist jealously enshrouds his secret, I recognise him as the cormorant fisherman, whose tradition and skills are almost as old and unchanged as the rocks and forest of hills that guard his forgotten world. Here the loud hubbub of the single cylinder agricultural vehicle, so synonymous with rural China, has not yet given way to the silent swish of the silver limousines.

I am not even writing from one of the show cities like

Shanghai or Beijing, lying along China's east coast, but from an inland city where, in the cauldron of time, mixed races have simmered down to the Han Chinese of today.

Crumbling, narrow roads meant for barrows and carts, have given way to six-lane highways that carve their way through the city. Here, overhead traffic lights count down the seconds to their change on digitally generated screens. Buried forever are the used taxis, imported from Hong Kong and Singapore. Now, numberless fleets of plush, aircon, Chinese-built cars sweep you effortlessly to every part of the city.

The highways are flanked not by the featureless apartment blocks of Chairman Mao's regime but by distinctive towers, in a subtle but dramatic weave of glass, steel, marble and granite, often incorporating the finest design features, both classic and modern, from the world's centres of civilisation. Tall and elegant they stand as a tribute to the young design architects who have worked for their PhDs at the universities of the great cities of the world and match the aspiration for homes and offices of China's emerging financial elite.

Its airports, like no others on the planet, are home base to the staggering array of new Chinese airlines, where 777 Boeings and 360 Airbuses seem to be everywhere! Double-decker aircon diesel sleeper trains thunder through day and night across distances akin to London to New York, crossing plains, deserts and mountain ranges with grace and ease. Similarly, new luxury sleeper coaches hurtle intercity road passengers around the growing motorway networks.

This is new China awakening, the most rapidly changing nation on earth. In its sheer scale of landmass and weight of population, in its bustling economy, in its advanced technology, in its military might, it strains towards the goal of unchallenged supremacy. China has redrawn the world map as the graphics on its overland coach fleet tell me loudly: *China is the centre of the world.* Not surprising, then, that its eager hands are outstretched for a giant's slice of the world's resources to maintain momentum towards its certain destiny of world domination.

Fifteen Minutes in a Modern Development Zone

The steel door of my flat closes heavily behind me, and its clunk sets aglow the stairway lights. The entrance door to the apartment block closes too, its coded lock a reminder that without a sharp memory I would spend the night outside. I walk through the gardens and acknowledge the men painting the kerbstones, trimming the shrubs and cutting the grass. Lady sweepers chase the dust that dares appear. Occasionally these ladies have very demanding work as the rain deposits the yellow sand, swept into the atmosphere by storms in the vastness of the Gobi Desert. Should I be bored on my short walk, classical music plays to me through the low-level lighting posts. Moments later, I am through the main gates where the security police acknowledge me in friendly gesture.

I take the only road that leads away from this small estate, and immediately my senses are accosted by colour. To my left is open parkland, the layout artistically crafted in the best Chinese cultural style. Multiplied thousands of potted flowering plants, mainly reds and golds, are filling the contoured landscape in such a way that the pedestrian gains the most dramatic view. Some sweep upwards towards an impeccably carved marble statue. Huge flower bowls adorn the pavements under the shade of leafy trees. Not a deadhead in sight! Winding paths that follow the contoured land invite the eye to view a boulder outcrop perfectly formed. Suddenly fountains appear, flinging themselves skyward. They surround further elegant white statues. It takes a moment to realise that the fountains rise and fall to the rhythm of music softly playing in the background. They are enhanced by colour when light begins to fade and the pavements become bathed by their own soft, reflected glow.

All seems to float in a landscape of manicured grass, which sweeps away to a backdrop of white arches and magnificent hanging red lanterns. Smartly uniformed, white-gloved security guards, discreet among the shrubs and trees, watch that no footfall deliberately flattens the grass and never should a piece of litter defile the ground.

To my right a garden of low shrubs, planted to follow a cunning design, conceals beds of red roses, heads nodding silently to the whispering breeze. These lead to the entrance of a block of luxury flats that dominate all others. This is no sharp-cornered, look-alike structure, but bow fronted and draped with balconies, like falling folds of silk. Later, orange floodlights will define its highlights against the black sky. I follow the red, white and yellow sculptured paving tiles at the foot of the tower block's marble steps. They feel different under my feet.

They lead to the wide crossing over a six-lane road, made easier by the outside lanes being separated from the inner four by even more shrubs. I notice a girl student about to cross, but hesitating. I follow the line of her gaze. In a few moments an elderly lady, still clad in her communist blue, would also be at the crossing. Strangers in person, age and possible dialect, the young girl took her arm and, matching her slow steps, gently led her across.

On the far side, in the shade of the tree-lined pavement, students sell small items, things they have made or grown interspersed with simple jewellery, key rings and penknives.

I stop to buy a pocketknife. Over a few pence good-natured haggling begins. It attracts a crowd. Someone at my elbow says, 'Hello, I am an English student. Can I help?' So another voice joins the haggling. I walk on with my new knife, full of the satisfaction of having paid the equivalent of 1½ pence less than the asking price. The student at my elbow is still there. 'Can I talk with you for ten minutes, or even five?' She told me she was studying at the Philosophical University. I clumsily misunderstood. Thinking she had said the Political University, I asked her if she had the presidency in sight. Not surprisingly, she did not understand either. True to her word, after five minutes trotting alongside, maintaining a steady stream of English, she said goodbye —and that she would look for me on the pavement another day.

From where I stand, six universities surround me. Each day I walk the pavement, my eyes straining to spot a Chinese student, small, a slight build, long black hair and glasses. My description fits a hundred I could see at any time. I smile at them all, worried lest I should miss the special one.

The tree-lined pavement almost immediately leads into a huge marble and granite tiled square. Artistic excellence is inescapable in every direction. Its different heights, its low shrub walls, its impeccably smooth finish allow spontaneous groups of dance-loving old and young to swirl effortlessly in the music–filled, cool evening air. Exotic raised gardens of rocks, shrubs, flowers and palms secrete away even more fountains that rise and fall to the music that calls the hundreds to dance.

In the freedom of the open space, old men sit on small stools and enjoy boyhood again by miraculously flying giant kites in the still air. They are traditional Chinese shape and colour, and hold motionless in the free sky.

In interesting contrast, very young boys drive electric police cars and jeeps wherever they want to go while little girls in Barbie doll pink sports cars teasingly follow them. I pretend to take a picture of the tiniest boy perched on a plastic replica American traffic cop motorbike with howling siren. My eyes meet the watchful mother's gaze. I read her approval. Having taken courage, another mother pushes forward her older son, who stiffly approaches me. 'Hello, where do you come from?' asks a white face in a flat monotone, the melodious song of Mandarin lost in the tension of the moment.

'I come from the country of Wales,' I answer in stilted English.

His face does not light with recognition of having understood, but follows with, 'Thank you velly much.' He turns and skips back to his mother with a relief that borders on joyful glee. His whole demeanour is now exuberant with personal achievement, and so is that of his mother, who understands even less.

For myself, I have enjoyed this moment's interlude. The mother's silent gestures, nods and smiles loudly speak out her appreciation across the cultural difference that separates us. In return, I have the satisfaction of knowing that I have brought her a present from Wales she could not have dreamed of. Forevermore, she will now be able to tell the story of how her darling son, so small and afraid, first talked to the lanky, long nosed foreigner ...in his own language.

A young couple approach me. The man wants to take his girlfriend's photograph standing alongside me. I oblige. I walk the square, conscious that a large dragon's mouth is lining up to swallow me. It advances to within a few feet before it slithers away, perhaps deciding against the taste of a foreigner. I see a serious-faced small boy peering from behind its sword-like fangs, his hands clutching tightly the small handlebars by which he steers it. Following it, not nearly as frightening, is a giant grasshopper, and a little girl steers a giant panda. I should not have been alarmed for, to the other side of me, I see children astride elephants, bears and even a tiger with flashing eyes and crunching jaws, walking with mechanised gait. All obediently walk, halt and turn to the power of tiny hands that tug on a small pair of handlebars, as much to the enjoyment of parents who stand by as to the children. Perhaps I am seeing a good feature of China's one child policy.

Elegant shops and restaurants, too, have their space, not in crushing weight, but sensitively guiding the vision via more flights of marble steps to the elevated palace of digital marvels. The electronic market is the show house and outlet for world-leading, ultra-sophisticated electric power and technology.

Guided by yet another hundred yard long line of swishing fountains, my passage across the square leads through an arch hanging with giant red lanterns, into a long precinct of shops and restaurants, divided down the centre by bronze casts of shoppers, flowers, trees and – guess what? – a circular island of fountains, silvered by halogen lights.

Unexpectedly, into this fantasy world, where old men and children can change roles and where parents can dream, I hear the crackle of gunfire. Suddenly, toy cars stop whining and the children stand up in them and look. I follow their gaze and pretend to be at least as brave as they are. Under a smoky blue haze I see what looks like an enormous orange reptile thrashing around in its own death throes. It is actually exploding inch by inch towards its own tail. It had been tightly packed with firecrackers. The sounds are of battle, but fought with an invisible enemy. It is an offensive against the world of dark demon forces. Under the shadow of the palace of hi-tech achievement, a new shop is opening. The position of the building has been spiritually determined, the placing of the idol shelf meticulously ordered, the size of the idol calculated and now the building's demons are considered to have been scattered. It is thought that the success and profitability of the shop depend on the co-operation of unseen allies in the spiritual world.

I spot a hairdresser and make a mental note to pay a visit the next day. I wish I had not done so. From the pages of a glossy book, I choose the style I wanted. I need not have bothered, for everyone comes out with the Chinese equivalent of a short back and sides. If I follow my inner compulsion, I will head straight to the nearest wig shop!

Coloured floor lighting diverts my steps to the stairway that invites me to an elevated balcony of shops and restaurants, with bridges that arch the balconies either side of the precinct.

The orange fireball is low in the sky and I stand to watch it dip into the city skyline, and to welcome the cool tide of dark that has already entered the precinct below. The area will soon be awash with leisurely strollers relaxing in the night air. A young male, smartly dressed, escorting three young females, approaches me. He calls to the three ladies to watch him offer me his hand in a gesture of friendship. So as not to ruin his little game, known to men the world over, I play along, accept his invitation and rise to stand alongside him. Though his breath tells me he is acting out of false courage, the females are impressed. One searches her handbag for a small camera while the others run to us to make a foursome. The photographer looks perplexed as her flash has failed to fire. She has not been able to enter into the fun of the moment. At the long, loud instruction of the male, she tries again. 'Three, two, one, go!' he commands in Mandarin —and the electrical eye has frozen the moment. We are all happy. In the final jabber of Mandarin, when all four speak at the same time, I think I understand one word: 'American.'

'British,' I correct them, and we part, still good friends.

My fifteen-minute journey ends comfortably at a small table overlooking the island of silver fountains. As I take my seat, I try to reason away feelings of sadness —that the spark of belonging which ignited between five human beings for two or three moments of time had died as quickly as it had appeared, and would probably never happen again. I consoled myself with the thought that at least one of us has a photograph that, for her at least, will be a key that can unlock the memory of a treasured instant.

Of course, I should emphasise that my fifteen minutes has described life as I have experienced it in the heart of a reasonably modern development zone. It is also a pleasant day in May, and summer's blaze has not yet singed the landscape.

As I leave the sculptured square tonight, I know that waiting at the exit point will be some of the most coolly expensive – and outrageously uneconomic – large foreign cars, tools in their owners' search for identity and status. All come with black livery and windows in darkened glass.

These will compete for space with the smaller imported cars and an array of Chinese-badged makes unknown to me. To these I can add the torrent of Chinese-made taxis with European marques that stop for fares as they drive by. Complementing the cars are the prodigious numbers and makes of motorcycles, a tribute to China's ability to respond to a market —they are already the world's largest producer. Finally, like an echo from old China, somewhere in the jostle for space will be the humble trishaw, a three-wheeled pedal cycle with a box at the rear for passengers, whose only brake is the trishaw man's foot against the front tyre. The passengers who await the trishaw have also a destination to reach ...which for the next fifteen minutes I will visit with them.

Fifteen Minutes in the Shadow of the Moon

The traffic thickens and the suffocating buildings give way to the open approach of the railway station; the rail travellers' journeys are over, mine is about to begin. What they know, and I am to discover, is that I am about to enter a quarter of the old city where probably only the rats outnumber the closely packed inhabitants.

The streets behind the high station wall are no more than broken surfaced, dimly lit pavement-less lanes, but these define the hub of this local community. Open-fronted shops, and eating places where the charcoal-fired wok never seems to cool, open onto a pool of muddy oily water where the lane should be. Everything is grubby, but the plates, slipped inside plastic bags, are piled high with noodles, bean sprouts, green vegetable and egg, smell good, and cost just 25 pence. Small, lit signs distinguish barbershop from teahouse where groups of men play cards on the floor. Wooden barrows offer fruit and vegetables that can be bargained for. There is thick dust on everything. A local man – small, round, flip-flops, black shorts and black-striped tee shirt – has a carrier bag dangling from one hand. The surroundings apart, for all the world like an Asian visitor on holiday, with a loud voice he begins to extol to the barrow ladies the virtues of the foreigner. They smile to each other and utter something unintelligible even to a Mandarin speaker. Undeterred, he continues booming, and with gesticulating fingers claims that, like the foreigners, he too is a university graduate and understands these things. He is paying me a compliment that is untrue. Not even my shadow has darkened a university door. It seems he is deranged, so we quietly ease away. He thinks we need to hear more, so he follows us.

We turn into a smaller lane. There are no more shop signs and the lighting grows dim. These are single-room dwellings, perhaps three storeys high. Iron doors flank either side of the lane, which is barely five feet wide. The lane leads on and on. Some men are sitting on doorsteps. One shouts and follows us; his attitude is aggressive. A sudden opening in the wall leads us deeper into the maze. It is a dark, broken uneven lane, hardly three feet wide in places. Similar rows of iron doors line either side. The glow from a solitary light bulb that hangs from its wire against a wall is the only light. Despite its restrictions, this lane has constant use. It is a passageway to the communal toilets. They have no water and may not lead to sewers.

I look through a half open door. The room is unkempt; a small, well-used moped leans against a wall; the remainder is given over to gambling. Light sneaks through a door, in anticipation of our arrival. A tall, white-haired, seventy-three year old Chinese man welcomes us. His face does not carry the interesting creases of old age but is white and drawn. If I am not mistaken, he has the look of someone who suffers with his lungs; a look which would have identified some of the old coal miners in Wales. This room is clean. It is rented by my colleague and given to the old man to aid his recovery from life on the street. There is a bed, but little mattress; two stools, a gas ring and a light bulb, a plastic bowl with some water, but no food or heat. We have brought him some noodles straight from the wok, but he declines to eat them, saying he will be really hungry by tomorrow.

We have the key of another door, next to the gambling room with the moped. This room, too, is clean, apart from the paint that flakes from the walls. Save for one stool, a few bags of used clothes and a light bulb, this room is empty. I sit on the floor, lean on my rucksack against the wall, and wait.

Sound echoes around this lane, for there is nowhere for it to escape. The mind automatically tries to fit sound to sights that are familiar, but here I fail miserably. In an unusual dialect, a one-legged man with a crutch negotiating the broken passageway, who is calling for a dog which is snapping furiously from within the toilet area, defeats my attempt. From a second floor room with an open window, a woman's voice cries out. I decide that she is in pain. Later I learn that she is deaf and cannot hear the sounds she makes. Then a sound I do recognise, the street advocate for foreigners has not lost our trail, and now he is clamouring to come in. Opening the door just a crack was enough. He knew where to push and there was no break in his tirade, though this time he is pointing at some barrow ladies only he could see. We turn him around and hustle him out of the door. He does not resist but retreats back up the lane, perhaps calling on the deities to shore up his cause. These are 'inner China's' streets and dwellings. Often there is no income; there is no social security, no medical care, no lighting, no heating, no clothes and no food, save for that earned by scavenging from waste bins. And these are inner China's better off.

Outside their doors, bolted against the uncertainties of the dark lane, sits, or more accurately, lives Lazarus —many of them, huddled together or sometimes in isolation within a greater isolation. There were more before winter had moved north. These have not experienced the respite of spring this year. Starving, wet, frozen men, women and children have slipped lonely into the final night of death. Among the survivors there are the wounded. A hand or foot that became exposed during sleep, froze. Gangrene has set in. Now a hand drips its fingers or half a foot is rotting away towards the ankle. The black flesh carries the smell of putrefaction. Often the redeeming features of such wounds are the maggots that keep the red flesh clean.

Yet the spaces and belongings of the dead are soon taken over by the living, who will move from where there has been trouble or where conditions were unable to sustain them. There is the construction worker who fell on a metal spike that ripped through his foot, shattering his bone. Dismissed by his employer with only travel fare back to his city, his family could not accept responsibility for him. Sitting in the streets, bracing himself against the pain, he watched his foot fester and swell and, unable to help himself, he starved. My colleagues discovered him and arranged his hospital treatment and finally the amputation of his leg below the knee. Back on the streets he physically recovered, and with it his spirit recovered also, and he soon worked out how to employ himself. Yet there is another, his foot destroyed by frostbite, who began to make a recovery until the police brought a charge against him; he fled —choosing the pain and isolation with freedom for at least a short lifespan, rather than the remoteness of a prison cell.

Tonight we meet a new arrival, without shoes —both feet are bound into some kind of sock. He says that both had deeply frozen. Curious unhelpful onlookers hinder our inspection of the damage. We decide to return in a few days to help this man. When we do, and with the persuasions of other street people, we entice him into a taxi, and guess our way through the maze of alleys in the minority quarter of the city. At the Chinese clinic, the taxi driver insists on taking only half the fare. Our new friend, filthy with long, matted hair, scrabbles along the floor through the arched doorway into the courtyard. He is just thirty-four years old. People stop and stare. We wait until our doctor colleague is free. What he needs we buy from the pharmacy, and wound cleaning begins. Half of his left foot is missing, the toes perhaps chewed away by rats, or picked off and pocketed, in the hope of being used again; the bones to which they were attached protrude from a swollen sausage foot of rotten flesh. With him sitting on the ground, the doctor picks away the rot. The heels on both feet have rotted in the same way. Infection has spread widely. A plastic bag slowly fills with decomposed foot. A mixture of saltwater and iodine cleans the remaining flesh. Plaster and gauze pads and an old pair of slippers, suitably cut, complete the dressing. He understands he has to take the strong antibiotics we buy him. We return him to his place under the railway arch. While his dressings and slippers become the attraction of his street-sleeping friends, we buy him bottled water, some noodles, and say goodbye with a promise of another visit to the clinic tomorrow. Leaving him on the pavement to the monoxide fumes and the smell of urine seems cruel, but it is by actively using his wounds to beg that he can stay alive. Reducing him to dependency on us would be death of a different kind.

The following day he feels better. We hoist him up the stairs to the doctor's room. This time a cream is added to his wounds; it is the colour of what seaweed paste may look like. Bandages carried from the UK bind him up and stronger antibiotics are given. On the journey back to his few feet of pavement, he asks for a haircut. We hoist the grimy bundle through a hairdresser's door and hope for the best. Mouths hang open, payment is confirmed, and he is accepted. Never had hair that looked like this been washed here before! Later, as we walked away, leaving a lone figure sitting on his piece of pavement, his shiny crew-cut and white bandaged feet either end of a bundle of old clothes, I have the distinct feeling that his personal value, confidence and self-respect were beginning to re-emerge. After searching, we find a hospital that agrees to perform an amputation, but meanwhile we find that flies have found his wounds and maggots fill his bandages.

Not all have retained the spirit to live. Some, overcome by an act of kindness, weep the cry of despair. Others lift lifeless eyes, and silently an unwashed hand will reach out for whatever we have to give, the will to speak lost in the death of motivation.

Another, not yet abandoned by the fleeting shadow of self-respect, eases his embarrassment by drawing a calloused hand across his face. It has the opposite effect. It draws attention to the tumour within his skull, protruding through the eye socket. He had been keen for a medical opinion, only to hear himself pronounced as beyond help.

This time, it seems he has undergone some kind of cauterisation, which had left a protruding black mess. Perhaps he has been glad of what medical help he could find, from the little money he could make from the sale of used coke cans and plastic bottles from the railway litter bins.

We spot an eight year old abandoned boy. He catches our eyes and makes off frightened, dodging between people, and slips into an underpass. We follow him with food and love, but he is nowhere to be seen. Doubtless he has found others like himself. These are probably among the hundreds of abandoned children clinging to life wherever they can find shelter.

Against a wall at the end of an unlit lane, the remains of an ancient easy chair, rotten from exposure, still rests where it has been dumped. A heap of ragged bedding lies alongside. Nothing in the alley misses the gaze of the small figure sunk into the seat.

In the gathering darkness he makes his way to us. Hand outstretched, he greets everyone. The light dancing in his eyes tells all we need to know. He quickly gathers some of the bags and carries them ahead, leading us to more like himself. Realising I am a stranger in his world of underground passages and narrow alleys, he places a guiding hand on my arm. His face, lined with a smile, conveys a concern his lips cannot voice, for he is dumb.

We enter a tunnel that has been home to a father and daughter. They walked here from the country. She will attend school each day while father collects cans, bottles and newspapers to support themselves. This underpass has now been cleared of street people, save two who share the same space, as neither have legs. A flap of skin also covers an empty socket where the older man's arm should have hung.

33

Forced beyond modesty, their toilet is where they lay. They are dependent on those who share similar poverty for even a plastic bottle of contaminated water. The old man, with uncut hair and heavily lined face, seems to be in a state of constant shock. If at all, they seldom speak.

I reflect on the old man's wounds. At one time a badly wounded old soldier perhaps? Not knowing where it may end, I close down that line of thinking, for I too had been a soldier, fighting communist insurgents. Perhaps, those years ago, could he and I have been fighting in the same conflict, but on different sides? Now the young and old take refuge in each other. They converse without speech, and had agreed that being two, though badly disabled, they might discourage the theft of their important ragged bedding before the approaching frozen steel of next winter.

Fighting conflict within myself, I lingered near the old man I supposed had been a soldier. However, what only hidden knowledge could record was that as the moments passed they were bringing me to an appointment I had not made. I looked back at a sound I did not recognise. A lady, poorly dressed, pushed ahead of her a homemade, wooden, small-wheeled handcart. It had once been painted white, but now the worn edges wore black grime. Standing in the cart, tiny hands gripping the sides, an excited small boy was unable to keep still. At the sound of the wheels the old man sat forward also, and spring appeared on his lined face. He wriggled his head and the little boy danced with delight. At the sounds of the old man's 'Bo! Bo! Bo!', he chuckled even more. The lady rushed her cart by, oblivious of the miracle that had taken place. The little boy looked back and the old man bent forward. They held their eye contact until the cart turned the bend at the tunnel exit.

A desert holds few surprises as amazing as the ibervillea plant. For seven years it may look like a piece of unattached driftwood. Then, at a few drops of rain, it sends out shoots and bears fruit. Here, between the concrete walls of a tunnel somewhere under the city, was no less a miracle. A drop of water in the form of a baby boy, broke the silent despair in the old man. I hoped his spring would find its summer in this prison under the earth, where the sun cannot be seen, nor its warmth felt.

* * *

The rising cold through the stone floor earthed my wandering mind back into the bare room where I sat and waited. The iron door that locked out the street, the naked light bulb that burned yellow, the flaking paint on the damp walls, the rucksack against which I leaned, were again my realities.

The stone wall was a poor barrier against the sounds of the mah-jong players in the next room. Their shouts and the clatter of their pieces on the makeshift table brought to mind images of my past years on China's streets.

* * *

Before the rail network that covers China's vast and varied landscape was linked by the wonder of computer power, I had to wait three days midway on a train journey. The first leg completed, it took several days of queuing and haggling at a ticket window before the second leg could begin.

Meanwhile we had sorted out some cheap hotel rooms next to a communist convention centre in a small town where foreigners were not welcome or perhaps not even allowed.

Later, we were a little unnerved to discover that a convention was actually in progress at the time. That evening we made an exploratory visit of the area.

I had already seen some of the local abandoned children, indescribably dirty, dressed in rags, hiding in a drain near the railway station. I understood their fear of daylight, as I had watched the security guards with rubber truncheons discipline the waiting ticket line. This prepared me for what the evening unfolded.

I stepped back onto a grass verge to allow official cars to sweep into the convention centre and realised that I was among others who were using the verge that night. I could see a number of young and older men in blue communist work clothing, sitting or lying among the shrubs and trees. Save for one, who lay between the pavement and the road. Under the day's blaze of the sun and the heat of the ground, no longer able to sweat, his mummified skin had shrunk tightly over the bones of his face, stretching his mouth and eyes wide open; his skeletal flailing arms gesturing helplessness as they moved from his mouth to his body. Those who passed detoured and stared from a distance. Without comfort, among people but alone, under the harsh glare of security lighting, with grating car gears within feet of his body and in the sight of those who watched with curiosity, exhausted he surrendered his final battle.

Among the remaining, a young man sat and stared at his dying friend. Eyes and mouth wide open, his face wore a similar mask. My colleague returned quickly to the hotel, warmed a cup of milk, pressed it into his hands and helped him raise it to his lips. There was a flicker of response but he managed no more than a sip. We continued our walk along the partially lit road. When we returned, the boy and his dead friend remained unmoved. The only change was that the cup of milk had been stolen.

The hour was late. My colleagues returned to the hotel. I decided to continue alone in the other direction where there were some oil-lit food barrows parked on the pavement. Within a few hundred yards, movement among the shadows of the shrubs in the dark verge again caught my eye. A figure of a man, face down, dragged himself along the grass towards the pavement. I looked for some place where the privacy of darkness could surround me, where I could sit, think and watch. I saw the same man. He had dragged his sick body to the food barrow. His skeletal figure was making a plea for help that could not be mistaken. The violent language of the barrowman and the boot that followed were also a message the starving man could not ignore. It seemed to take him forever to pull himself across the pavement to the protection of the grass and shrubs once more.

Others in less severe condition than the man on the floor hovered in the darkness beyond the reach of the oil lamp's light.

The following morning, before the strength of the sun struck the convention hall courtyard, a hundred or more delegates assembled in the open space. Three or four leaders dressed totally in black, swirling curved swords, led them through the daily spiritual and practical routine of t'ai chi.

The blue-dressed lady pavement sweepers had been out early and had collected the dust and litter in their carts. The grass verge and the shrubs looked as if last night's tragedy had been a dream. Not a man remained. It could never have happened... except for the corpse. It had been swept free from the pavement and now shared the road with the traffic. A drone of flies over its head, some already feasting on the eyes, others in the tunnel of an open throat.

On the morning of the third day, tickets secured, we set off on the walk to join the boarding queues at the railway station. Unthinkingly, we looked towards the point where the corpse had lain the night before. There had been no major change apart from – either out of respect or disgust – someone had placed a communist newspaper over its head. We turned to leave as the government cars began to swish into the car park and the t'ai chi leaders waited quietly to lead the decision makers into good form for the day. Rightly so! For the little town's centre has been cleared of housing, and erected in its place is the highest statue on earth of Chairman Mao, with his fixed smile, his raised hand and outstretched arm, blessing the nation's poor.

* * *

China is an economic success story —but at what price to its own people? To some extent it feeds off itself. The majority of its labour force comes from the country, their only value being what they can produce. Behind the colossal reconstruction work is a manual workforce, slaves of progress, with little income, without rights, discarded when they can no longer produce.

I visited an empty building that had become home to a labouring workforce; ten or twelve men, crowded bunks in unbelievably tiny, foul-smelling rooms without water, toilets, heating or medical facility. However, better than the pavement, the underpass or the ducting for hot water pipes where the abandoned children sleep.

Knowing of the traumatic effect of the unequally enforced one child policy, I listened while one of my street friends talked of his family. 'We were four children,' he said. 'My two sisters were given away.' He did not go on to say if he were the brother who was also rejected. Villages are raided and houses searched for additional children. Large fines are imposed where they are found or else they will have no schooling or any rights of citizenship. Without status of any kind, they enter the labour market or live on the streets.

What of girls? I mused. They are normally the first abandoned, but the horror of my experience in Taiwan froze further thinking. At first glance, Taipei could be thought of as a city of barbershops, until I was told that they thinly disguised the workplace of some seventy thousand young girls, many from the indigenous hill people, contracted out by their families to the Chinese city gangs for five-year periods.

An unconscious antipathy towards hairdressers had caused me to frown at the extraordinary number of them in one street. At twenty-five I gave up counting as I noticed in each one a friendly staff member or two, responding to my interest... always young ladies provocatively dressed!

Heatedly, I argued with a colleague. 'Surely they can escape, fly away —to Britain, perhaps?'

'Maybe,' she agreed. Then, after a few minutes, she added, 'If they are sold on, they could join the flow of illegal immigrants, but under the tight control of others.'

'What is their value?'

'I read of a fifteen year old sold on for £4,000.'

I walked on in shocked silence, turning over in my mind the disjointed pieces of our conversation. I thought of the fake passports, said to cost £15,000; the yearly visa, for which more money would have to be provided; the danger of employment without any documentation; the risks of disease and injury; and the hazards facing the families, especially any other daughters.... Then I thought of the British low-life sharks who choose their time to make their own pickings, adding to the sorrow of those who have no tears left to cry. I reflected on all this and much more. But this is another story waiting to be told.

A soft knock on the iron door and a drawing of the bolt broke into my thoughts and brought me back to the little room. A medium-height, thin man hobbled in. One leg, significantly shorter than the other, hung almost uselessly as did his arm. His face, set with a survivor's wisdom, was bright with recognition and appreciation. He appeared like light that chooses an unexpected part of the landscape. Under fire from starvation and winter's icy blasting winds, without regard to his own safety, he cared for others on the street, when despair had savaged their will to live. Were he a hero of war, he would have earned recognition, but now, with his back against the wall, he slid to the floor opposite me.

Another joined us, and another. A young man brought his elderly mother; she had a painful leg ulcer. They have had to abandon their home in the country and huddle each night in an alley. For half an hour they continue to come. For one evening in the week, Lazarus comes in from the gate and amid the flaking paint and under the bare hanging bulb, he sits on the cold stone floor of the rich man's house and... dreams. A young man, his face alight, eager to help the more distressed, had come from the country to find work. His wife was ill and she needed medical care. Perhaps until winter's chill set in he would survive the streets. Captured by stories of wealth in the city, he had used their precious reserve on the train fare to come and work for it. When the night was over, standing proud, he walked off, not looking back. Perhaps we made a mistake not helping him find that work when it had been in our power to do so.

The world of harsh reality is limited; the world of dream's imagination is boundless, and the future might just lie in that direction. In tonight's hour where the positive power of hope fills the room, some may be encouraged to take their first step in the direction only their inner eyes can see.

Sitting with them in this house of dreams, I found it easy to dream also. I was thrilled by being able to enter the world of possibility that lay entirely outside my ability to bring it about. For I am aware that I dream because our great Creator dreams, and in this sense at least I am made in His likeness. In fact I am convinced that He allows us to dream a little of His greater dream of a world of people willingly wedded to Himself.

Yet my dream arouses an unsettling fear in me also. Here I dress simply in Chinese style, yet when one enters this little room, their eyes flick my way. I am easily recognised as a foreigner. These people are China's embarrassment —not meant for foreign eyes. I have been aware of how harshly they are treated, on the streets, on the square, but it is what happens out of sight that makes me shudder. I wonder how long we will have a little room in which dreams can be refuelled. It is so important, for already some have begun to share their dream and the hope that arises from it with others on the streets. Sadly, I did not realise that the reality of what could happen had already begun to close in on me.

The Final Fifteen Minutes:
A Total Eclipse

A student confided in me. 'It is difficult for us now. We have had thirty friends arrested recently.' A sense of foreboding deepened. That evening, a phone call that did not say much, other than we could expect a visit —after dark.

Meanwhile a group of foreigners are busy. Emails and phone calls fly in many directions, careless of the consequences. In a few hours they will be thirty-five thousand feet above trouble, heading into the Western world where their unscheduled departure, suitably adapted and embellished, will become the latest taste to titillate wide-eyed, sensation-hungry friends and even church groups. They belong to a culture where, without cost to themselves, in an explosion of vanity, purposefully leaked information about their sudden departure, then a careful explanation as to why the need to be silent, will be enough to stoke the fire of imagination. This will turn curious travellers into heroes, but only in the unreality of a make-believe world. The reality would remain in China, where the true cost-counting had just begun, and where some of my colleagues would be among those who would pick up the bill.

***

My first insights into the practice of faith among the Chinese population had begun some years ago when I had been asked to meet some Taiwanese young people who were about to cross the border from mainland China into Hong Kong. Eventually, four very young Chinese appeared, poorly dressed, not a little dirty and without personal belongings save a small canvas shoulder bag. In a small cottage amid the New Territory rice fields, they would rest up, wash, change clothes and then continue to Taiwan. Eventually, my inexperience of China began to show in the callous way I broke a cardinal rule by asking them what they had been doing. In a hoarse voice, the leader replied, 'Teaching a group.'

'What size group?' I continued.

Embarrassed he replied, 'One hundred and twenty.'

With condescending false graciousness I responded, 'That's a large number of people.'

He did not raise his head, nor even glance at me, but under his breath said, 'One hundred and twenty thousand.' I was stunned into silence. My initiation into the underground church in China had begun, and I felt that one step better than the ground opening and swallowing me would be to become a disciple to my young friends.

The driving force that had motivated them to learn all they could in Taiwan then to carry it into China was their

Christian faith. They explained that free, unfettered faith, like the wind, could blow over villages and cities, over desert and mountain communities, touching each person differently as it passes. No-one has control of the wind. No-one can tell where it comes from or to where it flies. Faith is the sunlight that causes spiritual life to bud, flower and bear fruit. It is the invisible substance that gives firm attachment to God, and by means of faith, eternal realities invade time's space. The invitation of the Chinese was, 'Come and help us strengthen faith.' My young friends had responded and, under cover of night, hundreds of people would gather at appointed farmhouses.

***

Since then, time has chosen to enlarge my experience. I have learned to live comfortably in underground community, and with the pressure of being sought for —even to within yards of my hiding place, and to the point of the seeming blindness of my pursuers.

'Mei Li, where are you going, you are barely sixteen? Rong Rong, Hong Mei, are you going too?'

'We are going north of the Yellow River, teacher, where there are few who believe.'

'When will you return?' I asked.

Mei Li turned away, her eyes fixed in a stare as if it were not the bare stones of the barn walls that had stolen her gaze. Muffled sobbing filled the silence without disturbing it. Among the group, a young woman was feeling the pain of an imprisoned husband and another of an imprisoned father. When quiet returned, I looked again at Mei Li. She did not volunteer an answer, at least not with words, for words might have squeezed her into a framework she did not want. It was the silence that answered me with an accuracy unknown to words. 'Perhaps ...never!'

The luxurious world of 747 jets which had roared me into Beijing in as many hours as it took months some time ago, or even years at one time, was beyond the experience and maybe even the imagination of Mei Li, but not so the two-wheeled tractor that had hauled us to the farm the night before.

I had learned to look for eye contact in a crowd and had begun to follow the man who threaded his way to a quiet street. Dusk helped blur our connection. A parked van, its sliding door a few inches open, was an invitation to enter. I clunked the door behind me and crouched on a seat below the window line. Three hours into the dark we stopped. Hardly visible, an anonymous tractor awaited us. The sound of rustling canvas guided us; we slid underneath it. The tractor, if it can be called that, was no more than a primitive engine balanced over two wheels; the trailer it was hitched to provided the other two. A hand that wore its broken nails and tough calloused skin with dignity, cranked the great flywheel which persuaded the single-cylinder motor to reach for life.

Within yards we no longer existed, swallowed by the night, the rain and the vast featureless space. Only the tractor driver was to know our destination. A murmur of Mandarin, the opening of heavy gates and farmyard smells, brought to an end the hour or more of open fields, stony tracks and watery ditches. Twice we had become bogged down.

What I had not realised was that the suspension-less trailer and sheet were a luxury that a hundred others, their feet heavy with mud, their bodies whipped by rain, did not enjoy as they tramped towards dawn and the same destination.

The canvas sheet raised, the invitation of an open door, warm green tea, an iron bed with a thin mattress, a blanket and... sleep that seemed to mock my aching body and torment my questioning mind.

Who is the man who is sharing his room with me? He is a leader; prison has already claimed six years of his life. I felt like an impostor into his private space. Why does he lie on his bed fully clothed? There is only one blanket and it covers me.

Why does he crouch silently on the boards of his iron-framed bed an hour before dawn, his lips moving but no sound forming? He is in an intercession for the day that awaits our living, and perhaps it includes me.

Why is our room next to the low walled, door-less, roofless toilets, where stepping-stones are placed amongst the human waste? Why, this is where waste is stored for feeding to the hungry land and to the pigs that need to be fattened... it is also the most unlikely place for the police to hunt for the foreigner!

A hundred hungry mouths munched their way through whole boiled cicadas and rubbery steamed balls of dough. This was breakfast and the hour was 5 a.m. I have feasted on fat caterpillars with grass as a vegetable in similar circumstances in Africa. While neither appeal to the Western palate, I felt no temptation to wish for a high-class hotel room and the traditional banquet in honour of the visiting speaker. This is where I find value.

After two hours of subdued personal worship and prayer, teaching was to begin by 7 a.m. One hundred entered the barn and made space for themselves where fifty would have been a crowd. There was no furniture; each sat on the stone floor. At that point the lookout reported that, under the pretext of enforcing one child policy, the PSB had raided the village searching for illegal children ...or could it be for us? The barn door slammed on a hundred suffocating people who made no sound or movement for eight hours. In a smaller room, hidden behind cupboards, my colleagues and I also waited out the hours. When the police retired, teaching began.

This police diversion served me well. It helped me find a beginning with a people time seemed to have ignored, but whom I desperately wanted to serve. I wondered what place my prepared studies would have in life as explosively dangerous as this. They were yesterday's meat, canned and reopened. My heart told me, 'Tear up your notes' —but my reason was afraid. I think I compromised.

On the third and final day, the village was raided once more. Each one froze for a further six hours. It was only when the aggressive invasion and interrogation halted at the house next door, with the PSB standing outside the walls that hid us, that they gave up their search. As they drove out of the village, the teaching recommenced.

Finally, the commissioning of the new young missionaries began and small teams stepped forward according to the towns and provinces to which they were being sent.

It was not the tears that filled my eyes, nor the emotion that shook my body, that caused me to stumble over the words of my prayer as I laid hands on the heads of Mei Li and her friends. Rather, I was frantically searching within myself for words equal to the occasion, but finding none. These silken bunches of black hair were calling for something I could not give, but I knew where they could find it... hidden in the longings of Jesus Christ.

Sadly, the kneeling figures would never know the wealth of new meaning they were adding to my life, as they exposed me to the mystery of learning from those you serve. Neither would they ever know that I was disregarding every rule of 'sending procedures as per the handbook' —that after reading this some may think ought to be written!

'How many of you work like this?' I asked.

'Many thousand,' came the reply. 'We are from a network of three million,' another said.

'How long will they enjoy freedom?' I asked.

'Three years,' said one.

'Three months,' said another.

'Some of them pray and will not touch food until they make their first disciple,' said someone.

Yet no statistics include them and no familiar structures enfold them. Suddenly, Western domination of the world Christian league tables looked thin and fragile.

I began to feel glad that the barrier of language had saved them from understanding the words I had prayed over them, for they could be trapped by my mindset. I wanted them to be free to explore life beyond them. If anything, I would have liked my words to point them to the silence in the spaces between them, for that is where God may be heard.

As had happened on the path between the rice paddies with my young Taiwanese friends, I ventured outside the safety of my personal cultural and spiritual interpretation, the invisible environment I live and breathe. I had, in an extraordinary way, entered theirs, and breathed the air of their faith —and for a fleeting instant, I understood them. That moment indelibly marked a stage in my own history from which I cannot retreat. Faith is the soil as essential to spiritual life as earth is to our planetary life. Everything that has life grows from it. In the most ancient wisdom of the kings, it was the Syrian general, made wise by faith, who asked for a gift of two mule-loads of earth to take back to his own land. The song of the soil of faith welcomed me, but the little bunches of black silken hair never knew.

My heart was singing, but my lead-like feet reluctantly turned to carry me back to the lands where faith is confused with belief, where sometimes the popular usage of religious vocabulary peaks with the words, 'You cannot do it.'

With the onset of evening we melted into the back of a waiting vehicle and began to slither our way along the mud track. As I had not viewed the farm from the outside, I glanced back at the massive wooden gates, the high stone walls and the solitary tree from which the song of cicadas had grown significantly less as the days passed.

It was then that I noticed something that set off in me the deep chuckle I needed to release me back to life outside those severe walls. Written across one wall, emblazoned in characters of red, was a saying of Chairman Mao. It extolled the virtue of hard work and of the Chairman's generous and wise leadership!

What is it there for? I thought. No one reads it. The villagers know it by heart and there are rarely any visitors. Yet.... could it have been the reason the PSB had stopped searching for us right outside these very walls? As we slid our way into the night, changed vehicles and drivers at a secret location, and watched our guide dissolve back into the crowd, I wondered at the earthy wisdom of these unknown Chinese, and at what might be its parallel law in the spiritual world.

The consequence of expressing faith, freely and lovingly, in hidden communities, with full knowledge of the severe terms of imprisonment that can follow, is essential to keep alive faith's true nature which, like a stream, runs along the bed of the individual's willingness to follow the promptings of the heart. Faith seems to capitalise on the latent force of the real person within every man. It is faith's humble men and women who will be seeds blown by the wind over Chinese borders into a waiting world.

Certainly China has an officially registered church, tolerated by an atheistic government. This has become an effective means of reducing the free nature of faith into a harmless, static, controllable structure —a structure of religious belief that becomes the executioner of faith.

* * *

My thoughts turned again to my Chinese late-night visitor. He and a companion had been asked to aid a foreign group visiting north east China, until the PSB had raided their rooms, a video camera recording all their reactions. Under interrogation, my Chinese colleague was shown the information on the foreign leader's laptop: dates, places, names. He could only hang his head and say nothing. 'At my next interrogation,' said my friend, 'I will give nothing away.' Meanwhile, homes have been abandoned, families uprooted, for by the time of the second interrogation, mobile phones, messages, texts, cameras, laptops and notebooks would have all yielded their evidence. Hungry prison doors stand ajar and those likely to be interned are among the forerunners of what could be the greatest missionary advance of all time.

* * *

The night visit touched a raw nerve in me, tendered by the suffering of an African friend already three years into a prison sentence without charge while his family outside .... wait. Then there are the group of associate Chinese leaders, each of them having served at least two prison terms of three years. Their leader, a man of my own age... five prison terms, a total of fifteen years; and the saintly ninety-one year old lady, whose face seems to smile at me when I most need encouragement, who served a single term of twenty years!

Emotionally bleeding the dark blood of sorrow, I wanted to weep, but instead it turned to anger. The foreign group, in the strength of their belief in the right of might, had invaded this private underground world with devastating results.

An unsolicited comment by a taxi driver voiced the growing conviction. 'Foreigners —ugh! They are so proud, they think that they have the right to interfere in everyone's country —just as they did in Iraq!'

Not knowing what better to do, I left my flat and turned in the direction of the old quarter of the city and walked and walked. This was my China, the land that had adopted me, the nation that had given me new life. I wanted to feel in touch with its people again. Their joys I have freely shared, their sorrows I had begun to taste.

I agonised over the mindless consolation I had attempted to express to my suffering colleague. It was a vain attempt to cover up the fact that my shallow experience had not allowed me to relate to his position. The attitude I did not hold, the understanding I did not have, the things I did not say, the prayer I did not pray, the action I did not take, were hammering me into despair.

I crossed the boundary of the economic development zone and headed into the maze of narrow, broken and grubby streets; before me the open-fronted shops, some offering little apart from bringing the shopkeeper into the life that was lived on the pavement, where there was one.

An elderly granny lies asleep in a chair with the street cat asleep on her lap. There is no pavement, so the trishaw man, his three-wheeled vehicle loaded with empty baskets and cardboard, negotiates around her in the narrow roadway. Squatting card players, oblivious to everything except the turn of the next worn card, take up fully half the road space. The trishaw man does not seem to mind. As he passes, he looks over the shoulders and viewing their hands of cards, joins in the game.

Gradually the pace of my walking slackened as my anger subsided. The streets of old China were once again having their calming effect on me. There was a small cloud rising over the horizon of my memory. It was no more than a wisp, but it began reminding me that the issues I faced were not new. A writer had used the experience of a lone priest some four hundred years ago, to highlight a similar incident, bringing the moral aspect into fine focus.

* * *

The priest had sat on his heels in a small cell, each wall within his arms' reach. Its earth floor was bare, a small grating in a wooden door his only source of light. The air was foul. He sat with his back to the faint light source and stared at the black wall, day after day, the only interruption, some grains of rice or a piece of rotten fish every two days. All he can see are the pictures that play in his mind.

He was not a curious retired traveller. Since leaving

Europe, the journey of this missionary priest had taken three years. Under the cover of dark, he waded ashore without money or possessions, hoping it was Asia's black sea that pounded the rocks. These were the years of ferocious persecutions of Christian believers. He knew that he would be easy prey, for possibly he would be the only priest alive in this land and a notable prize for the magistrate leading the inquisition.

Against the blackness of the cell wall, vivid images from the past formed on the inside of his closed eyelids. Betrayal in the form of a professing believer had led him to a village. He could recall the deathly silence of the village sounds as the guards marched in. He could see from his hiding place, tiny tufts of black strung together as the betrayer and two leading men, both volunteers, were led away for interrogation. The betrayer was freed, while the village elders were chained to stakes at the low reach of the tide. They took many days to die.

The images his eyelids brought back to him did not hold the horror now as they had done at first, for his mind was wrestling with something more profoundly despairing. He lived through the torture and execution of three more villagers who were bound into baskets and by a lance prodded over the side of a boat to sink in the cold black waves.

Worst of all, when physically and emotionally broken, he hammered on the door of his cell for the sounds of the night were destroying the last threads of his sanity. The guards seemed to be waiting for his response as through the grid they told him the sounds were not snoring as he had thought, but the moaning of three more village men who had for some days had been roped tightly and were hanging upside down in a pit. 'Oh they have done nothing wrong,' laughed the guard, 'but they suffer until you choose to revoke your confession of faith.'

The priest had slumped back on the earth floor. In the thick blackness of the night and in the inner darkness of his world, one shaft of penetrating light reached back to the hard benches of his seminary years and to the religious culture he had woven around himself. It had helped him find his inner bearing and set the course of his own destiny. He would leave his own safe shores and die for the people of Asia. Now his layers of bookish knowledge were as thin as fragile parchment and about to tear. For the reality that immersed him was that his coming was the cause of others suffering. In fact he had not died for them, but they were dying for him because he had come!

***

My final fifteen minutes are over and I am feeling depressed. This tempts me to open a package of thought I had already labelled 'Not to be opened until the last day', but here it is.... In a couple of weeks another jumbo will slip unnoticed into the sky at the start of its westward trek. With it, there go I, filling an economy seat... having been among the worst of those who have offended China.

I turn to leave my comfortable old city streets —and from a pavement barrow buy some dried banana slices. With the packet in my hand I begin to feel better. Amid the Chinese characters and pictures of bananas, in English, I read: *Good Quality, Nutsitive And Delicious Feeling Of Metsopolis Sense Of Happiness*. 'Mmmmm, must be good,' I thought, and absentmindedly slipped one into my mouth. The slices tasted as if they had been fried in fish oil!

Ah well, few things are as they appear to be, for this is unfathomable China, and it is still the country of people I love.

Epilogue:
Footprints in the Yellow River

It was early in the morning as I walked up the steps cut into the steep hillside. The sun, already a fireball, was sending searching probes into the valley. At the dragon's gate I stop, lean on a parapet and look down onto the waking town. It had already largely disappeared. A classical Chinese green-tiled roof with turned-up eaves, surreal in the drifting mist, helped me identify a university that I knew, snuggled into the foot of the mountain. Somewhere out there, in the corridor between the heights, the timeless Yellow River swung in an arc on its irresistible passage to the sea. Local people call it Mother Yellow River, as Chinese civilisation found its identity here and was nurtured along its banks.

Though still relatively early, the dragon gate and its surrounding compound is busy. Many people have walked this far up the hillside; some carry leafy tree branches and breathe in their healing properties. The elderly gently work their t'ai chi routines. Others have continued up the hill, but are walking backwards! Far more serious, an older man of slight build stands before me; his outstretched arm holds a heavy, curved Saladin-style sword. It points directly at my forehead. His black judo dress and look of total concentration alarm me. As if in a trance, he guides the sword and, with sweeping motions, begins to pattern the air. Two sandaled feet shuffle in my direction. I move to one side, but his fixed gaze does not follow me. I hear the horrifying thud of the sword as it dissects the air. The breath of it passing ruffles my hair. The swordsman completes his action, turns and looks at me... as if I were not there. I relax when the flashing metal returns peacefully to the leather scabbard.

It is a further two hours' climb to the ancient pagoda on the summit. As we step out, like the Titanic the tower blocks in the valley below lose their definition and sink in the sea of mist washing over the valley floor... only it is not mist, but dust-filled polluted air, spewed into the atmosphere from the remorseless output of the factories. Like an advancing tide, it builds steadily until the valley looks filled with thick sediment at the bottom of the sky. People, cars and even buildings melt away into its grey nothingness and the wide river gives up its trickle of the sun. Eyes become inflamed, sinuses block and breathing becomes difficult. The idol shelf is dusted and the divinity implored that a wind may sweep through the valley and a respite be enjoyed. Ah, wait until China's promised six hundred new coal-fired power stations come on line, then global warming will become more than an interesting theory, as air pollution reaches pandemic proportions.

The summit is cooled by a refreshing breeze and a poorly-clad lady from a minority race leads us to where she has placed some chairs in the shade of a few hardy trees. I look down into the teacup she has placed before me. Green tea I recognise, but this has whole flowers and dried fruit swirling on its surface. More like the Sargasso Sea, I think to myself, as I attempt to sink the vegetation.

We rested and chatted as we sipped our tea and I nibbled its rehydrated contents. After the inevitable photo session, where some of the Chinese girls dressed up in Mongolian national costume, the men decided to walk back down the mountain. The ladies, however, in a display of feminine wisdom, elected against the hundreds of steps and dusty trails in the unforgiving sun, in favour of a taxi ride back to town.

Ping had been a stranger up until two days before when he had accosted me on the street with his friendly 'hello'. He was a primary school English teacher and had welcomed the invitation to join us on our day on the mountain. We had begun to enjoy his company also; his openhearted honesty was refreshing. 'I am sorry,' he said, 'that I do not have faith.'

'Most Chinese people would not have faith either,' I stumbled over my response, and was relieved when the conversation changed. An hour or more later, we were again at the dragon gate, the town now beginning to come into view through the shroud of pollution. We leaned on the parapet, breathed again the lustreless yellow air, and let the time drift by, unwilling that our walk and the pleasure of each other's company should end.

Again, the honest childlike openness of Ping took me by surprise. 'Do you think that I could have a Bible?' he asked.

In a small street market at the foot of the hill near the spot where we had met up earlier that morning, as the darkness of night began to mix with the colours of the day, we prepared to part company. With simple directness, it was Ping who spoke out once again. He said, 'I would like to have your faith, too.'

Later that night we met once again and, over a meal together, made him a presentation of the Bible he had asked for... confirming him in his newfound faith, and myself in the wonder of how purely and easily faith had come to its place in the heart of this Chinese man.

All generations of China's sights and sounds have been played out on the banks of a silent, endless river. Old drawings show a generation living in cobbled streets, wooden houses and shops and gateways, with architecture as wild as the wind in the blue ice peaks. But the river remains unchanged.

When I first visited this province and walked among the generation whose turn it is to be alive, I followed the river between its crossing points. It seemed to me as if the yellow waters were made up of the tears of the yellow soil that was sorrowful in its long wait to feel the footprints in its dust of those who would redeem it to its rightful inheritance. I wept with the river, and my tears added an infinitesimal weight to its flow and my prayer a droplet to an eternal intercession. The river was silent, but it is in the weight of its silence that the force of the immaterial stirs.

China is in its second long march, for which the first was no more than a rehearsal. The silent river flows with purpose. Perhaps we are now in the countdown to their economic, political and military domination. In the absence of faith, this would be a terrifying destiny for the remaining world.

However, my forty-five minutes has introduced me to the highflying student elite force, whose pure faith has tempered the hungry pursuit of materialism; to the hope of faith among the Lazarus population, whose lonely deathbed is the roadside and the footfalls of the unconcerned; to the outlawed and imprisoned, whose only crime is to experience the reality of their faith, perfected through suffering. I have seen the holy purity of faith demonstrated by Ping, who joined me to climb a mountain, but who in reality climbed an inner Everest and descended forever a changed man.

Faith laughs at the limitations of political and religious structures. It enjoys the freedom of the wind to affect the whole spread of society. So I feel confirmed in my view that the tide of this nation's irresistible advance will carry with it seeds of wild faith, depositing them wherever they are received.

As the flame of the western dying sun streaks blood-red among the layered clouds, so they mischievously wisp and curl fearlessly among its cooling embers. These are like lawless images in the sky that grow in their confidence at the decaying empire of the sun's wasting day.

The colours of the emblem of our past colonial Christian heritage engage fruitlessly with the encroaching night before they are lowered in surrender.

In the western night, it is towards the east where the sky confuses with the land that the faint glow of the sun's flame begins to halo the earth's rim. It signals its visit to another continent to awaken its sleeping people.

My spent minutes captured memory of an eastern dawn as I had lived through its present reality. So I am about to return to Wales, to close my notepad and cap my pen... when I am stabbed by words I did not want to hear: more foreigners have surfaced in the area and engage my Chinese colleagues.

I do not know how I should feel, so a hatch in my mind slams shut. Inwardly, my anger begins to rise. I am jealous for the safety of my Chinese and other friends.

The spirit of colonialism subtly resurrects itself. It suggests that 'we' are endued with spiritual qualities while 'they' are the natives. But it is an arthritic hand that we hold out, for we mistakenly believe that, like discarded clothes, faith is a 'hand down' from a failing Western church.

We have yet to understand that China's faith is not the creation of an existing system of religious belief, but stands in its own elemental purity, inspiration and newness. Pure faith is no less than the gift of God. Faith is not meant to pour the life of its own future into a known mould... the stale offering of the sinking West.

Searching for words, I find only an inward cry. 'O God, not again.'

* * *

Losing my poise, I withdraw into myself and become silent. It is for this space hidden wisdom waits, and gently leads me to the vault where memory is stored until its appointed time. In a holy quiet I hear a Chinese voice say, 'When the second interrogation begins, I will be silent. Whatever happens to me I will not give away anyone.'

I recognise the voice, and with heart pounding I say to the air, 'These are the words my Chinese colleague spoke at our secret late-night meeting.' As so often happens, I spoke too quickly, and before the air had the chance to receive my words, a deeper prompting contradicted me. 'No,' it said, 'these were the words that faith spoke —thinly disguised in your colleague's voice.'

My frustration fell away and the inner warmth of faith began to glow in its place.... This is what China is like!

A Personal Invitation
from the Author

Like the song of an incoming tide, accents of Korean, Chinese, Japanese, Egyptian, Tigrinya, Arabic, German, Polish, Kurdish, Iraqi and Portuguese dash against the rocks of familiar English and somewhere in the medley, my Welsh accent also searches for a space.

This is not a central cosmopolitan city, but a tiny south Wales town near the spot where the spark of the 1904 Welsh Revival ignited.

If I had thought of Wales as a land without significance, now I understand that the erosion of time has no effect on divine purpose.

The spiritual eruption that volcanoed into the Welsh Revival has now passed out of range of human experience, its lean monuments starved of praise; like Wales' ancient stone megaliths, they topple —and, as with people, they are reclaimed by patient earth.

Not so divine purpose. It is as if its energy still strains for release. I stand on Llanelli's Machynys, the legendary

'Monks Island', now home to a new international golf course, and wonder if the vision of the vibrant Celtic monastic life of Wales and the prayer that arose from the many Welsh revivals, could be drawn from the same source of divine purpose. If so, then perhaps I have also found the reason why our own missionary vision has, over the past thirty years, been able to train and place hundreds of missionaries at the earth's farthest reaches, to say nothing of the new mission movements birthed and training centres opened. Perhaps it is also why our small, brave Llanelli town, lonely in its spiritual isolation, has a hidden significance.

This is the reality from which *Forty-five Minutes in China* has grown, though I am more than aware that my writing has not yet begun to reach the horizon of the page.

* * *

China is a nation where opportunities outnumber volunteers, a hundred to one. To sow life and energy into China is to do so where the most far-reaching investments can be made. Should you feel that China could be a challenge made for you, or if other aspects of the life and programme of *Nations* interests you, please get in touch with me at the address shown below.

Rowland Evans

Nations Trust,
International Centre, Glanmor Road, Llanelli,
Carmarthenshire SA15 2LU